GENETICS
THE SCIENCE OF LIFE

Cloning

SUSAN SCHAFER

Sharpe Focus
an imprint of M.E. Sharpe, Inc.

Sharpe Focus
An imprint of M.E. Sharpe, Inc.
80 Business Park Drive
Armonk, NY 10504
www.sharpe-focus.com

Library of Congress Cataloging-in-Publication Data

Schafer, Susan.
  Cloning / Susan Schafer.
      p. cm.—(Genetics: the science of life)
  Includes bibliographical references and index.
  ISBN 978-0-7656-8138-6 (hardcover : alk. paper)
  1. Cloning—Juvenile literature. 2. Human cloning—Juvenile literature.
I. Title.
  QH442.2.S34 2009
  176--dc22
                              2008008115

Editor: Peter Mavrikis
Production Manager: Henrietta Toth
Editorial Assistant and Photo Research: Alison Morretta
Program Coordinator: Cathy Prisco
Design: Patrice Sheridan
Line Art: FoxBytes

Printed in Malaysia

9 8 7 6 5 4 3 2 1

Contents

Tiny aquatic animals called hydra reproduce asexually by a process called budding. The buds, which are miniature replicas or clones of the parent, grow out the parent's body and eventually break off.

CHAPTER 1

Can't You Just Send My Clone to School?

The alarm is ringing in your ears, screaming like a banshee for you to get up. You cover your head with your pillow. If you just had a clone of yourself, you could send it to school in your place. Or could you? Even if scientists were cloning humans, you would never be able to use a clone as your substitute, because your clone would be born a baby and you would still be a teenager. As your clone grew, so would you. You and the clone would always be the same number of years apart.

A **clone** is a cell or organism that is genetically identical to the cell or organism from which it was made. Cloning is a form of **asexual reproduction** because all of the deoxyribonucleic acid (DNA) comes from the same parent. People often think of clones as being cranked out of factories just as cars are, in order to take over the world. But clones do not have to be copies of whole organisms. An **organism** is a living thing. It grows, uses energy, responds, reproduces, and has DNA in its cells. So scientists might clone just the DNA, or part of the DNA, from an organism. Or they might clone just one type of cell, some tissue, or even an organ.

Regardless of what is being cloned, the process always involves DNA. DNA contains the genes or chemical instructions that tell cells what to do,

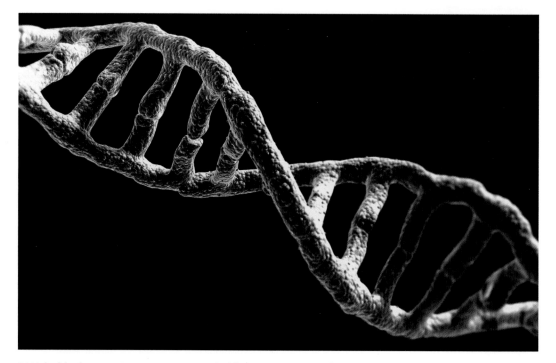

DNA holds the genetic instructions needed for an organism to function.

sort of like your parents telling you to get up in the morning. Each gene is one special type of instruction. Genes are found in DNA, DNA is found in chromosomes, and chromosomes are found inside the nucleus of a cell.

Scientists clone in order to make as many copies of genes, cells, tissues, organs, or organisms as possible, so that they have a number of samples to study. This way, they do not have to wait for natural processes to produce what they need in order to study diseases or develop new medicines. It is like looking for a needle in a haystack. If there is only one needle, it would take a while. But if there are thousands of needles, finding one would not take as long.

A BRIEF HISTORY OF CLONING

A German scientist named Hans Spemann created the first artificial clone in the laboratory in 1902. He used a human hair to split a two-celled

DOWNLOAD

- An identical twin is a natural clone.
- Cloning is a form of asexual reproduction that does not require two parents to produce young.
- DNA contains the genes that carry the instructions for building new cells.
- In nuclear transfer, the nucleus of a donor cell (with all of its DNA) is taken out of its own cell and put into a different cell that has had its nucleus removed.
- The first clone of a mammal was a sheep named Dolly.

salamander **embryo** into two individual cells. Each cell grew into the identical twin of the other. By doing this, he proved that each cell in a new embryo carries all the DNA needed to create a whole new organism.

Spemann was also the first to perform a **nuclear transfer** using embryonic cells, opening the doors for later cloning work. In nuclear transfer, a nucleus is removed from one cell and put into a different cell. By the 1960s, scientists were using the adult body cells of frogs to perform nuclear transfers. Then in 1996, the world was introduced to Dolly. Created by Ian Wilmut and Keith Campbell at the Roslin

German scientist Hans Spemann performed the first nuclear transfers, thereby setting the stage for future work in cloning.

Dolly, the first cloned mammal, was able to mate naturally, giving birth to a healthy lamb named Bonnie.

Institute in Scotland, Dolly was the first mammal to be cloned from an adult body cell, using the frozen udder cell of an adult sheep. The udder is the bag-like sac that holds milk glands in cows, sheep, and goats. Although Dolly was a clone, she gave birth to a lamb named Bonnie in 1998. Bonnie was conceived naturally, proving that clones can breed and produce healthy young.

A L E R T !

Cloning may be hazardous to your health. Most clones do not survive. Scientists tried more than 270 times before Dolly the sheep was finally cloned. After suffering from health problems associated with premature aging, such as arthritis and pneumonia, Dolly finally had to be put to sleep. She was only 6 years old. Most sheep live 11 to 16 years. Although scientists do not know if Dolly's ailments were related to her cloning, some are still concerned that using DNA from adult cells makes the clone start out with older cells, so they age faster.

Dolly the sheep, before she died at age 6.

THREE TYPES OF ARTIFICIAL CLONING

Scientists have developed three different kinds of cloning: DNA, reproductive, and therapeutic. DNA cloning involves individual genes or groups of genes. Reproductive cloning produces whole organisms, and therapeutic cloning creates parts of organisms.

DNA Cloning

For DNA cloning, scientists use living cells, such as **bacteria**, to transfer genes from one individual into the cells of another. A bacterium has normal DNA, but it also has an extra piece of DNA called a **plasmid**. When the bacterium reproduces, it copies its normal DNA as well as its plasmid.

Scientists have learned how to use plasmids to add new genes to bacterial cells. First, scientists use a special chemical that acts like a pair of scissors to snip the DNA they want to clone from a plant or animal. Then they use another chemical to cut apart the plasmid, which normally forms

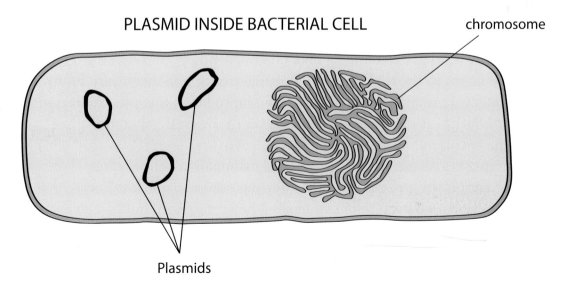

PLASMID INSIDE BACTERIAL CELL   chromosome

Plasmids

Most bacteria have one long, circular strand of DNA, as well as small extra pieces of DNA called *plasmids*.

RECOMBINANT DNA

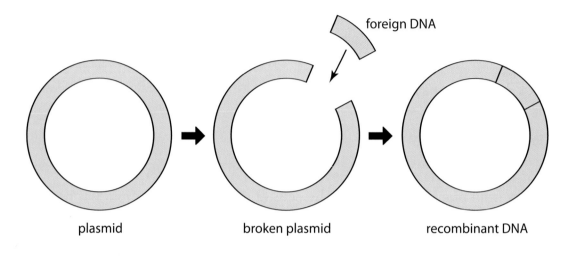

plasmid	broken plasmid	recombinant DNA

Recombinant DNA is prepared in the laboratory by breaking up and splicing together DNA from more than one source.

a complete circle like a rubber band. When the new DNA is added to the cell, it joins with the broken plasmid.

The newly combined DNA is called **recombinant DNA**, because the new gene or genes have been combined in a new way, with the DNA in the plasmid. It is similar to taking a bike chain, cutting it, and sticking a new piece of chain in the middle before putting it back together again. From then on, every time the altered bacterium reproduces, it copies the recombinant DNA in its plasmid and passes it on to the next generation. The bacteria become cloning factories for the scientists!

Scientists also use viruses, yeasts, and **mammalian** cells to clone, but bacteria are often preferred because they reproduce so quickly. Every 20 minutes or so, one bacterium can make 2 new bacteria. Those 2 can each make 2 more, or a total of 4. Four produce 8, 8 produce 16, and so on. The population doubles every time the bacteria reproduce. In just a few days, tens of thousands of new bacteria, all of them carrying clones of the introduced DNA, can be made in the laboratory for scientists to study.

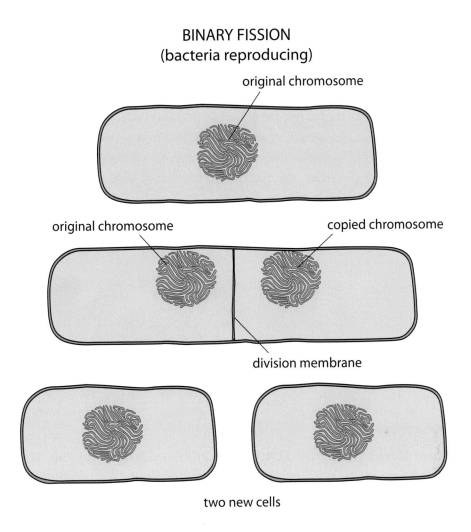

Binary fission in bacteria is a simple form of cell division.

Reproductive Cloning

In reproductive cloning, scientists take all of the genes from a cell and use them to make a copy of an entire organism. Using the method called nuclear transfer, scientists remove the nucleus from an adult donor cell and inject it into an "empty" cell, usually an egg cell. The egg is not really empty. It still has all of the cell parts that it needs, such as mitochondria to produce energy, but its nucleus (with all of its DNA) has been removed.

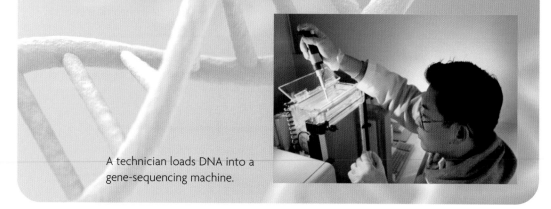

A gene machine is a computer program used to identify a gene that a scientist may want to clone. Genes in the DNA are made of special chemicals, called bases. The bases are arranged in different sequences to form messages, just as the letters in an alphabet are used to form different sentences. Each gene has its own unique message, so scientists need to be able to identify the right one. Gene machines work faster than earlier methods, speeding up the identification process.

A technician loads DNA into a gene-sequencing machine.

The egg no longer has instructions, so it will need a new nucleus as soon as possible. The needle used for nuclear transfer is so small that scientists have to use a microscope to guide it.

Once the donor DNA has been injected into the empty egg, it is zapped with electricity or treated with chemicals to make the newly created cell begin dividing. Once the cluster of new cells is large enough, it can be put into the uterus of a surrogate or substitute mother, where it will continue to grow until it is born. Presto—a clone!

Reproductive cloning was a breakthrough in science. Prior to its discovery, scientists believed that once a body cell had formed, it could never be any other kind of cell. Once a skin cell, always a skin cell, so to speak. As an individual grows, cells become specialized for particular jobs and some of their genes stop working or are "turned off." They are no longer needed. For example, if a cell becomes a skin cell, then it no longer needs to use the genes that cause a heart cell to beat.

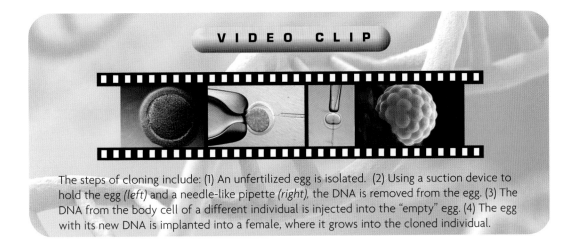

VIDEO CLIP

The steps of cloning include: (1) An unfertilized egg is isolated. (2) Using a suction device to hold the egg *(left)* and a needle-like pipette *(right),* the DNA is removed from the egg. (3) The DNA from the body cell of a different individual is injected into the "empty" egg. (4) The egg with its new DNA is implanted into a female, where it grows into the cloned individual.

Scientists believed that genes could not be turned on again once they had been turned off. But with new breakthroughs in cloning, they found that a skin cell, an udder cell, or any other kind of body cell could become a whole new organism. In other words, genes that were turned off *could* be turned on again. However, scientists worry that turning on and off genes in newly cloned cells causes reprogramming problems, like a computer programmer gone wild. As a result, many clones develop diseases, are deformed, or die.

Therapeutic Cloning

In therapeutic cloning, only parts of an organism are created. Sometimes therapeutic cloning is called embryo cloning because the reproductive cloning process is begun, but the new clone is not allowed to grow for more than a few days. The cells are then harvested to create more cells, special tissues, or organs. Because this process does not allow the embryo to develop into an individual, a lot of people are against it. Scientists are now finding **stem cells** in the bodies of adults that can be used in cloning. They hope that embryos will no longer be needed.

Stem cells are not **differentiated** or specialized. In other words, many of their genes have not been turned on or off yet, so scientists can manipulate them like a potter with a lump of clay. The potter might shape a bowl, a plate, or a vase. Each item has a different job, but they all came from the same clay.

DIFFERENTIATED CELLS

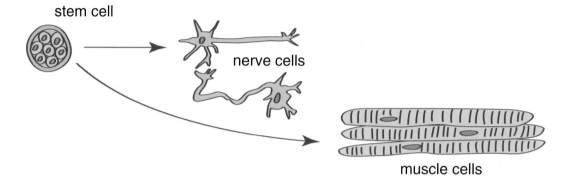

A stem cell has the genetic ability to change into any kind of specialized body cell.

Stem cells are like that clay. By turning genes on or off, scientists can turn a stem cell into any other kind of cell, such as a heart cell, a nerve cell, or a kidney cell. The new cells can then be used to grow new tissues, such as skin tissue for burn victims, or new organs for transplant patients. Patients would no longer have to wait for someone to die to get new organs, although until herds of animals are engineered to carry a ready supply of organs, potential transplant recipients may have to wait until those organs are grown. And their bodies would not reject the organs because they would be cloned from the cells of their own bodies. They would simply be replacing their diseased organ with a new one that would be created from their own cells.

CLONES ARE JUST IDENTICAL TWINS

Not all clones are created in labs. The word *clone* comes from the Greek word *klon*, which means twig. People have been cutting twigs from plants and sticking them in the ground to grow new plants for more than 2,000 years. They did not know it at the time, because they did not know about DNA, but the new plants were exact clones of the

One of the scientists who helped create Dolly, the first mammal clone, talks about using cloning to create healthier babies. By checking the DNA of very early embryos, doctors might be able to eliminate any defective cells and then clone the healthy cells before putting them back into the mother:

> Even when the technologies of nuclear transfer, genetic manipulation and stem cells have matured, I am sure that some people will still prefer to put up with the random insults of nature than be subject to human intervention, even if it is based on careful consideration of medical issues rather than whims. But at least they will have a choice and, for me, just having the chance to decide is paramount.
>
> —Ian Wilmut, in *After Dolly: The Uses and Misuses of Human Cloning* (2006)

Dr. Ian Wilmut sits with Dolly at the Roslin Institute in Scotland.

original plants. In fact, many plants and animals, such as the bacteria used by scientists to clone, reproduce asexually. Asexual reproduction does not require two parents. The organism simply makes a copy or a clone of itself.

Humans are cloned naturally when identical twins form. Identical twins occur when one fertilized cell divides in two, but instead of sticking together to make one person, the two new cells split apart. Each cell then continues to divide and grow into a different person, each with the same DNA.

It should be noted that whether created naturally or in a lab, clones are not really exactly alike. Once a clone is created, environmental factors, such as diet and experiences, can influence the characteristics of the individual. In addition, not all DNA is found in the nucleus of a cell. Some DNA is found outside of the nucleus in the mitochondria, the power plants of the cell. Lab clones only share the same nuclear DNA (from the nucleus of the donor cell), so they are even more different from each other than identical twins are. A clone's *mitochondrial* DNA is different because the nucleus is usually placed inside the cell of a different individual, not the original nuclear donor. Identical twins, because they come from the same cell, have the same nuclear *and* mitochondrial DNA.

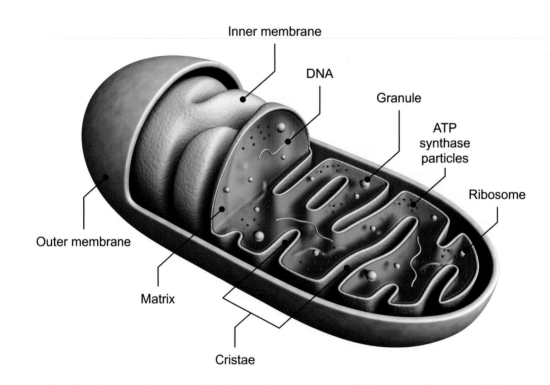

Mitochondria, the organelles responsible for producing energy in cells, have a small amount of their own DNA that is distinct from the DNA found in the nucleus.

With new technologies, lab clones are becoming even more different as scientists experiment with moving DNA from one organism into another. For example, a human gene that causes a disease might be put into the cloned egg (or even a naturally fertilized egg) of a mouse. Scientists could then study the human disease in the reborn mouse. A gene from a bacterium might be put into a plant. The bacterial gene improves the plant by making it more resistant to pests. The question becomes how far this "improvement" of organisms should be taken.

Scientists have discovered a gene responsible for decreasing appetite in mice, which resulted in weight loss. The discovery may lead to new treatments for obesity in humans.

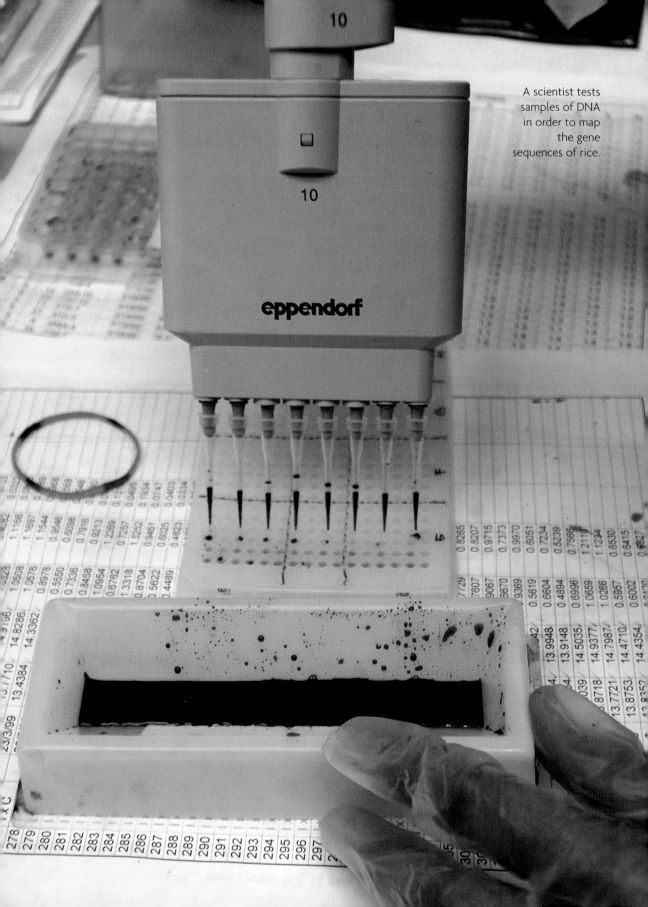

A scientist tests samples of DNA in order to map the gene sequences of rice.

CHAPTER 2

It Starts with a Cell

DNA is only found inside of a cell, and so all cloning begins with the cell. Whether scientists are interested in cloning one gene or many, an organ, or an entire organism, they must first locate the desired cell. Animal cells are now being studied extensively, but plant cells have long been on the list of genetically engineered, or artificially altered, species. **Genetic engineering** is the science that involves taking genes from one organism and putting them into another.

NEW AND IMPROVED?

When plants or animals receive genes from organisms that are of different species, they are called **transgenic**, which literally means *produced by transferring across*. The list of transgenic organisms is growing as scientists create mixed gene combinations in everything from tomatoes to goats.

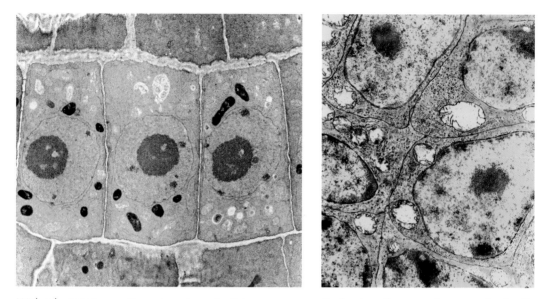

With advances in genetic engineering, scientists may soon routinely place the genes from an animal cell (*right*) into a plant cell (*left*), and vice versa, to produce desired traits.

Super Corn and Square Tomatoes

The United States leads the world in planting genetically engineered or so-called super crops. You may have eaten altered food or worn cloth made from modified plants without realizing it. Commonly modified super crops include corn, cotton, squash, soybeans, and canola.

Often, plants are engineered to produce a chemical that is distasteful or harmful to insect pests but not to people. If a plant has the ability to kill its own pests, then farmers do not have to use pesticides that are harmful to people and other living things in the environment. Other crops are modified to make them resistant to herbicides (poisons), which are sprayed on crops to inhibit weed growth. Plants also have been modified to slow down rotting rates or to increase vitamin content.

Rice is normally tan in color, but a genetically modified type of rice, called golden rice, carries the genes from daffodils. Once they are a part of the rice DNA, the daffodil genes produce the chemical beta-carotene, which gives carrots their orange color. The beta-carotene in the rice not only makes it look golden, but also makes it more nutritious. Beta-carotene

A variety of genetically modified corn *(left)* stands undamaged by the worms that can devastate crops of normal corn *(right)*.

is important because it is changed into vitamin A in the body, a vitamin that is important for vision and bone growth.

Fruits—such as strawberries, bananas, pineapples, sweet peppers, and tomatoes—have also been engineered to make them sweeter, more colorful, or less likely to rot. People are more likely to buy fruit with these characteristics. Modified "anti-rot" plants produce a smaller quantity of the chemicals that normally cause fruits to spoil. The fruit lasts longer after picking, which makes it less susceptible to bruising and squishing during shipment. Some scientists are even working on modifying tomatoes to make them

A scientist examines a variety of experimental golden rice, which has had its genes artificially manipulated.

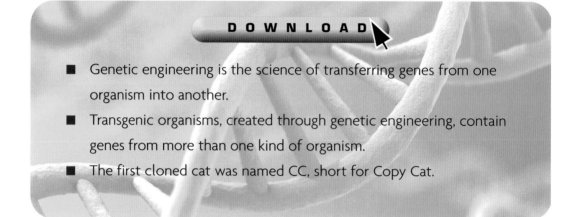

square. Square tomatoes would be easier to pack into shipping crates and more of them would fit, so farmers would save money on packaging.

Grow Fish

Meats from genetically modified animals are also being developed. One U.S. company has modified Atlantic salmon to grow faster than unmodified salmon by injecting them with genes from the Chinook salmon and another fish called the ocean pout. The modified salmon do not grow larger, just faster. Instead of taking three years to mature, they reach full size in about a year. Salmon farmers can produce more fish in less time, which saves money and provides more food for people.

The Chinook and pout genes are inserted into the fertilized eggs of the Atlantic salmon, so when they grow, the foreign genes become a part of every cell in the Atlantic fish. The gene from the Chinook controls the production of a growth **hormone**. The gene from the pout acts like a chemical switch that turns on the production of the Chinook hormone. Normally, Atlantic salmon only grow during the summer (their normal gene is activated by summer sunlight). Chinook salmon and ocean pout grow year-round. With their new genes, the modified Atlantic salmon also grow throughout the year, and therefore grow faster than normal.

Scientists believe the same technique could be used in other food fishes, such as trout. Opponents of the practice worry that genetically modified fish could cause allergic reactions in people (as yet unproven) or that altered fish could escape into the wild. Studies have shown that female salmon prefer larger males, which would mean they would prefer the modified fish to the wild fish. If modified fish escaped, fewer wild males would mate. In addition, modified males produce fewer young than wild males, which could lead to a decrease in salmon populations. The companies that produce the modified salmon, however, claim that this would not happen because they will only sell sterilized females (females that cannot produce eggs). Even if they escaped, they would not be able to breed.

In Japan, scientists are engineering fish in order to save endangered species, such as North American rainbow trout. Stem cells collected from mature trout are injected into the embryos of sterile Asian salmon. The salmon can be farm-raised, while breeding trout in fish farms is difficult. When the salmon mature, the males produce trout sperm and the females produce trout eggs. When the eggs are fertilized by the sperm, they grow into normal trout.

Glow Fish

Genetic engineering has even reached the pet trade. Scientists in Taiwan were the first to inject "glow" genes from a jellyfish into the fertilized eggs of tiny striped zebra fish. The glow genes are what cause a jellyfish to glow **fluorescent** green. When the zebra fish hatched and matured, they also glowed green. In another group of zebra fish, scientists injected a gene that causes coral to glow reddish pink. Those zebra fish glowed red. Now they are creating zebra fish with both genes, so the fish are half-fluorescent green and half-fluorescent red.

Many pet owners loved the novelty "glow" fish, but until recently the government would not allow them to be sold in the United States. As with the engineered salmon, opponents feared the fish might escape into the wild and endanger native fish populations. If crossbreeding took place, wild fish would glow and be easily picked off by predators. The distributors of glow fish also sterilize their fish, claiming they could not breed if they were to escape. Even so, some worry that the sterilization process is not 100 percent guaranteed, and one mistake could spell disaster.

Transgenic fish carry the fluorescent genes of a jellyfish.

Although popular as pets, glow fish were actually developed for medical research. Scientists use the jellyfish gene as a genetic marker, attaching it to the DNA of the cells that they study. The genetic marker allows them to see changes in the modified cells more easily, because they stand out next to the normal cells. Glow genes have been used to study heart development and track the spread of cancer, which could lead to new cancer treatments for humans. Scientists have developed glow pigs, glow mice, and glow insects.

Spider Goats and Enviropigs

In Canada, scientists have engineered goats with a spider gene that produces a protein found in spider silk. Spider webs are among the strongest known natural materials. When the goats produce milk, they also produce the spider web protein. The protein is **extracted**, or removed, from the milk and used to make ultra-strong containers, ropes, surgical sutures, and bullet-proof vests.

Another Canadian group has engineered what they call the "enviropig." The transgenic pigs produce feces, or manure, with less than half the phosphorus of that of a normal pig. Manure contains high levels of phosphorus because animals cannot easily digest or absorb it from the food they eat. As a result, it is a leading source of water pollution, running off into streams, ponds, and lakes, and killing wildlife. Phosphorus encourages the growth of algae, which reduces the amount of oxygen available to fish and other aquatic life that need it to survive.

The enviropig was created using genes from the bacterium *Escherichia coli* and from a mouse. From the bacterium, researchers took a gene that makes an enzyme that allows the pigs to digest and absorb phosphorus, thus reducing the amount put out in their manure. From the mouse, they took part of a gene that controls the production of **saliva** in the mouth. They injected the new genes into single-celled pig embryos, which were then

BLOG

Scientists in Canada have created environmentally friendly transgenic pigs, dubbed enviropigs, in an effort to lower the amount of water pollution caused by chemicals in their feces. In a news release, one of the creators of the enviropig said:

[The enviropig] is, for sure, the first modified farm animal engineered to solve an environmental problem.

—Professor Cecil Forsberg, Department of Microbiology, University of Guelph, 2001

implanted into female pigs. The transgenic pigs that were born produced phosphorus-digesting saliva. When they swallowed the saliva with their food, they were able to digest and absorb phosphorus into their bodies, leaving less in the manure.

Not only are enviropigs better for the environment, but also they save farmers money. Pigs need phosphorus to grow, but because normal pigs cannot absorb much, farmers have to pay for phosphorus supplements. In 2008, the Food and Drug Administration (FDA) announced that meat and milk from cloned pigs, cattle, and goats are safe to eat. However, only animals that are reproductively cloned have been approved. The approval was not extended to genetically engineered animals that carry genes from a different species. Scientists hope to show that the altered enviropigs are safe to eat because the pigs solve three problems at once by lowering pollution, saving money, and providing food for consumption. Other farm or ranch animals, such as chickens or cattle, could also be genetically altered to help the environment.

CLONING FOR AGRICULTURE

Once organisms were "improved" with new genes, scientists wanted a way to duplicate them. Conventional breeding creates new individuals with new mixtures of genes, half from the mother and half from the father. But scientists did not want variation; they wanted only improved organisms with the same new genes every time. So they cloned them, thus ensuring that the new genes would not be bred out.

Some farmers are using the same technique to ensure they get exact copies of their best farm animals. For example, they take their best cattle (those that produce desirable meat) or their best cows (those that produce the most and richest milk) and clone them. Instead of hoping that they will breed better livestock using regular breeding practices, cloning allows them to know exactly what they will get.

While reproductively cloned cattle have been approved for consumption by the FDA and studies have shown that their meat or milk is no different from that of normal cattle, some people are still concerned. They

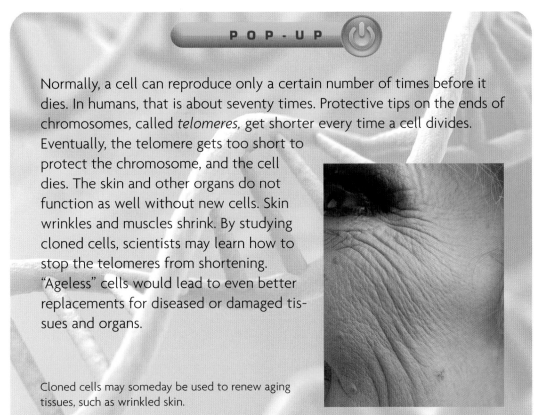

POP-UP

Normally, a cell can reproduce only a certain number of times before it dies. In humans, that is about seventy times. Protective tips on the ends of chromosomes, called *telomeres,* get shorter every time a cell divides. Eventually, the telomere gets too short to protect the chromosome, and the cell dies. The skin and other organs do not function as well without new cells. Skin wrinkles and muscles shrink. By studying cloned cells, scientists may learn how to stop the telomeres from shortening. "Ageless" cells would lead to even better replacements for diseased or damaged tissues and organs.

Cloned cells may someday be used to renew aging tissues, such as wrinkled skin.

especially worry that new genes in altered animals could cause allergic reactions. Others worry about the health of the clones. Do they get sick more often? Do they live as long? But farmers claim that the process is so expensive right now that cloned and genetically altered animals actually get better care than those that are not cloned.

In addition, studies have shown that cloned cows are not displaying the signs of premature aging that Dolly, the first cloned sheep, showed. The cows are cloned from older cells and yet their body cells appear to be as young as those of a newborn calf. Scientists hope that someday, if they can make old cells young again, they might be able to make replacement tissues and organs for aging people who suffer from heart failure or loss of brain function. The technology could turn out to be a "fountain of youth."

COPY CAT . . . COPY DOG, TOO

If cloning becomes commonplace, getting a cat or dog might never be the same. Instead of looking for a new pet, people could simply clone the one they lost. By collecting cells from a beloved pet at the end of its life, a genetic replica can be made.

In 2001, scientists at Texas A&M University were the first to successfully clone a cat. CC, which is short for Copy Cat, was created when the DNA from one cat (the donor) was inserted into the empty body cell (from an ovary) of a different cat. The cloned cell was then implanted into yet another cat, which became the surrogate or substitute mother.

BLOG

One of the scientists who cloned the first cat, CC, emphasizes that clones are not true substitutes for lost pets:

[T]his is reproduction, not resurrection.

—Duane Kraemer, Texas A&M University, 2002

Interestingly, CC's fur color was not exactly like that of the donor cat. This is because the environment in which an organism grows influences not only its personality but also how it looks.

The first successfully cloned cat, named Copy Cat or CC, is shown with her unrelated surrogate mother.

A kitten named Little Nicky was the first cat to be cloned for sale, at the request of a woman who wanted to replace her deceased cat.

For example, the diet of a mother can influence how the genes of a developing embryo are expressed even before it is born. Although a clone may be genetically identical to its DNA donor, it will never really be the same individual.

A private company in the United States offers pet-cloning services to the public. All you need is around $30,000. The first cloned-to-order pet was a kitten named Little Nicky. Little Nicky was cloned from the cells of a seventeen-year-old cat named Nicky, whose owner was grieving after the elderly pet passed away.

Cloning may soon be available to dog owners as well. In 2005, scientists in South Korea created the first cloned dog. Snuppy, short for Seoul National University puppy, was made from the skin cell of an Afghan hound, which was implanted into the empty egg of a yellow Labrador retriever. Although the scientists who created Snuppy are more interested in cloning as a way to study human diseases, a number of people are investing in dog-cloning research in the United States so that they can clone their pets.

Snuppy, the first dog clone *(right)*, with his genetic father *(left)*.

New techniques in cloning have created several generations of cloned mice.

CHAPTER 3

Cloning Humans

To date, scientists have cloned salamanders, frogs, mice, rats, rabbits, sheep, goats, pigs, cattle, horses, donkeys, mules, cats, dogs, and a type of monkey called a macaque. Could humans be far behind? Regardless of whether humans should or should not be cloned, many scientists agree that it is only a matter of time.

IT'S A NEW YOU

The first clone created by Hans Spemann was not a true clone. When he split a two-celled salamander embryo in two, he was really creating identical twins. But later, Spemann discovered that by removing the nucleus from one cell and placing it into another, some new development would take place. This was the beginning of true cloning, or nuclear transfer.

The first true clone was created in 1952, when scientists removed the nucleus from a frog egg and replaced it with a nucleus taken from a developing frog embryo. The resulting clone developed into a tadpole. Twenty years later, scientists did the same thing using cells from adult frogs instead of from embryos.

By the 1990s, large numbers of mice were being cloned. Then, clones were made from clones, which quickly yielded dozens of identical individuals. This was an important step because scientific studies are more reliable when performed on identical individuals. Scientists did not have to worry about whether the effect of a drug was due to the drug or to the individual variation that would be found in normal mice. In other words, they would not have to ask if a mouse reacted differently to a drug because of the drug or because it had different DNA than another mouse.

Clones, however, are all genetically identical, so anything that would affect one mouse would affect all of them the same way. With more identical individuals to study, researchers can learn more quickly how specific drugs, medicines, or treatments work.

As early as 2001, scientists were cloning early human embryos that were able to survive up to a six-cell stage. But in 2008, scientists at a U.S. company announced that they had cloned the first mature human embryos. Mature embryos have reached a stage in their development that makes it possible to implant them into a female. If this were done and an implant took hold, a cloned human could potentially be born. But that is not the company's intention. They want the cells for therapeutic cloning—to make replacement organs, such as skin for burn victims or kidneys for patients with kidney disease.

LIVING FACTORIES

In theraputic cloning, embryos only have to be grown to an early stage, forming a clump of about thirty or forty cells. The cells can then be genetically engineered to produce particular proteins, tissues, or organs as replacements in ailing people. The cells do not even have to be from humans. Transgenic animals can be created to carry human genes, acting as living factories to produce substances for treating illness.

A human gene is first inserted into a plasmid or a virus and then injected into the **zygote**, or fertilized egg, of an animal, such as a pig or cow. The human DNA becomes a permanent part of the animal's DNA. Whatever chemical instructions are on the human gene are carried out by the animal's

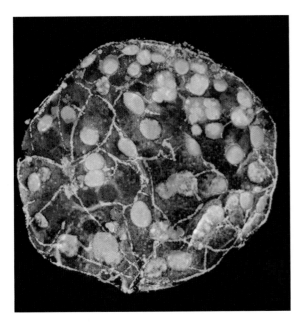

In its earliest stages, an embryo forms a clump of identical stem cells.

cells. As the zygote grows, every cell in the animal will carry the human DNA.

Scientists hope to use transgenic animals to mass-produce human proteins, such as insulin for treating **diabetes**. Diabetics cannot control the sugar level in their blood because their bodies do not make insulin. Manufacturers currently use genetically engineered bacteria to produce insulin, but animals like cows are bigger and therefore larger quantities of proteins can be extracted from their milk and blood. The result would be that more insulin could be made faster and more cheaply.

Scientists have already used cows to produce human **antibodies**, which are special proteins that help fight disease. Scientists took a human chromosome and removed all of its genes except for the ones that made antibodies. Then they injected the shortened chromosome into a cow cell, which was then fused with an empty cow egg. The resulting embryo was placed into a female cow. Every time the cells of the implanted embryo divided by **mitosis** (*my-toh-sis*), the human chromosome was passed along with the cow's chromosomes.

When the cloned calf was born, it carried the human chromosome in every one of its cells. The calf's cells used the genes on the human chromosome to make human antibodies, which were removed from the calf's blood. Several transgenic cows were made to carry the human chromosome, and scientists were relieved that none of them showed any side effects. All of the cows remained healthy in spite of the extra human chromosome.

Previously, only one gene at a time had been placed into cows, so each

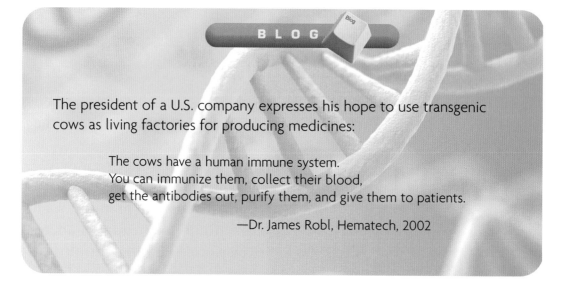

BLOG

The president of a U.S. company expresses his hope to use transgenic cows as living factories for producing medicines:

The cows have a human immune system.
You can immunize them, collect their blood,
get the antibodies out, purify them, and give them to patients.

—Dr. James Robl, Hematech, 2002

cow could only make one protein to fight one disease. By using a chromosome with many different antibody genes, a single cow could make many different antibodies.

An entire herd of cows has been cloned to carry the human milk gene. The cows then produce human milk in large quantities, which can be used to feed **premature** babies whose mothers are unable nurse them. Human infants have trouble digesting cow's milk, so the cow-produced human milk can also be used as a supplement by nursing mothers who do not produce enough milk of their own.

A lot of people are against using animals to create human products, so some scientists are trying to do the same thing in plants. They started by genetically engineering tobacco plants to carry the insulin gene of a mouse. The engineered plants produced insulin. The tobacco leaves were then ground up into a powder and fed to diabetic mice. Within eight weeks, the treated mice had normal sugar levels.

Now scientists have created transgenic lettuce that carries the human insulin gene. The modified lettuces produce human insulin. Insulin is normally given by injection, but the lettuce can be ground up, put inside a capsule, and swallowed like a pill. Lettuce can be mass-produced cheaply, and if the treatment works in human trials, millions of people with diabetes will be able to save money and avoid daily injections.

GROW ME A NEW ONE

Cloning is helping to grow new blood vessels in heart attack victims. It began with mice and pigs suffering from heart disease. Stem cells were injected into the animals' hearts. The cells took over for any injured or dead cells, which sped up the healing process of the heart.

Scientists then turned to humans with heart disease. Clogged blood vessels in diseased hearts keep oxygen-carrying blood from reaching heart muscle. Without oxygen, heart cells die. The heart fails, and the person suffers a heart attack.

To treat these patients, scientists cloned billions of identical copies of a gene that gives the body instructions to make blood vessels. Then, surgeons injected the genes directly into a patient's diseased heart. The genes went

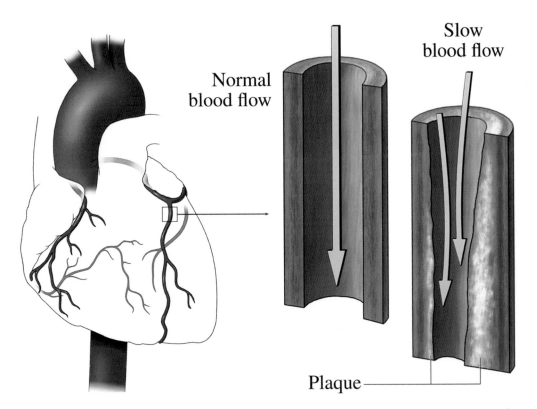

Plaque (*right*) that builds up inside of a blood vessel in the heart reduces blood flow, which can result in a heart attack.

to work, instructing heart cells to make new blood vessels. The new blood vessels bypassed the clogged vessels, bringing life-giving blood to the heart. Dozens of people with heart disease have been successfully treated using this method. The treatment is better than taking medications, which have to be taken long term, because once the new vessels grow, they are permanent.

Similar trials that used stem cells to grow new blood vessels for people with poor blood circulation in their legs because of diabetes have also been successful. Potentially, this gene therapy could be used to prevent gangrene, a condition that results when injured tissues lose their blood supply and die.

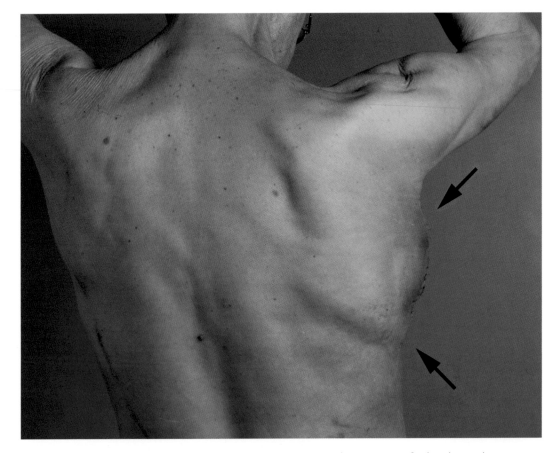

When a patient lost his lower jaw to cancer, scientists grew a replacement jaw for him by implanting a special cage seeded with stem cells under the skin of his back.

Fewer cases of gangrene would mean fewer amputations of fingers, arms, legs, or other extremities.

Scientists hope one day to grow entire organs as replacement parts. They have already successfully created human heart valves, bladders, and functioning replacement livers. Scientists have even grown new bone for a man who lost his lower jaw to cancer. Doctors took stem cells from the patient's own bone marrow and spread them onto a titanium mesh cage, which was shaped like a lower jaw. The inside of the cage was packed with the minerals and hormones needed to grow new bone. The cage was inserted under the skin of the patient's back. Because the stem cells were his own, his body did not reject them. Instead the stem cells formed a new jaw-bone, following the shape of the cage.

When the new jaw was fully formed, it was removed and transplanted into the patient's mouth. Soon after, the patient ate his first meal in nine years! In 1997, a scientist grew a human-shaped ear out of cow cartilage cells on the back of a mouse. Of course, the ear could not hear (hearing happens deep inside the ear canal), but the method could be used to make replacement parts—an ear, a nose, or a knee—for people born with birth defects or for those who have lost these parts due to injury, frostbite, or disease.

A laboratory-grown ear was successfully transplanted onto the back of a hairless mouse. The technique might someday be used to make replacement parts for humans.

Culturing Cells

When cells from an organism are grown in a laboratory, it is called **cell culture**. The cells that are created can then be studied. Animal embryos can be created outside of a living body in lab dishes this way. The nucleus from a body cell, such as a skin cell, is placed inside an empty egg and allowed to grow for a few days. Then about thirty or forty stem cells (cells that are not yet specialized) from inside the clump of cells are transferred to a culture dish. The culture dish contains a nutritious broth, called a culture medium, which provides the cells with the food they need to live and grow.

   The inner surface of the culture dish is lined with "feeder cells." Feeder cells are usually made from the skin cells of a mouse, which have been treated so they will not reproduce or divide. The feeder cells do not really

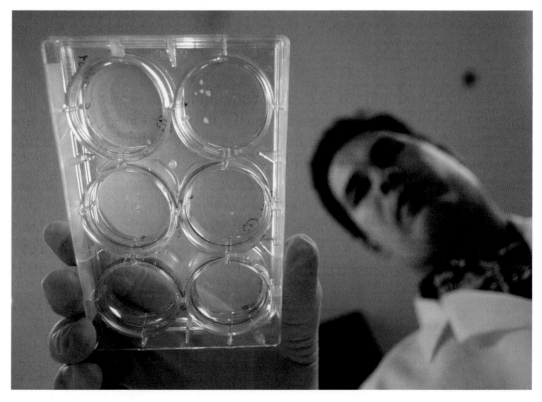

Scientists grow human stem cells in lab dishes for use in stem cell research.

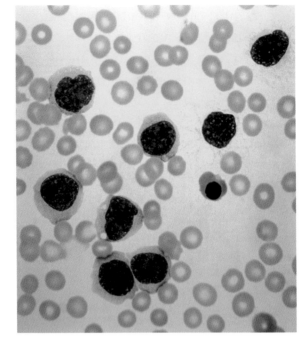

Leukemia is a disease in which the body produces a large number of abnormal white blood cells (stained dark purple at *right*).

"feed" the stem cells. That is the job of the culture medium. Feeder cells simply provide a stickier surface for the human cells to grow on.

When the stem cells multiply and begin to crowd the culture dish, they are transferred in small groups to more culture dishes, where they continue to grow. In this way, the original thirty or forty cells will grow into millions of cells. Potentially, they could grow forever.

After six months or so, if no abnormalities occur and if none of the cells have differentiated (turned into specific kinds of cells), the culture is accepted as an embryonic stem cell line. Scientists use cells from embryonic stem cell lines for research. Now scientists are looking for ways to grow stem cells, especially human stem cells, without using mouse cells. They want to be sure the human cells are never contaminated with mouse DNA or mouse viruses.

When researchers want to create specific kinds of cells, they change the culture medium that the stem cells are growing in. By using specific chemicals to turn particular genes on and off, they can grow different kinds of cells, such as nerve cells, heart cells, or blood cells. Scientists can insert specific genes into the cells to get them to change. Many scientists are culturing human cells because they can be used to treat diseases or injuries. Nerve cells might help someone with a spine injury. Heart cells might treat patients with failing hearts.

Stem cells are also important because scientists can use them to test new drugs and treatments. If they use human stem cells, the way the cells react tells scientists more about how certain drugs might work in the human body. One day, it might be possible to custom-tailor stem cells to treat individual patients with specific ailments.

Work has already begun in using cell cultures to cure cancer. Patients with leukemia, a type of blood cancer, have been successfully treated with stem cells. Their cancers went into total **remission**, which means that the patients no longer showed symptoms of the disease. Some tumors, as well as cancers of the pancreas and ovaries, have also been treated successfully in this way.

See the Light

Stem cells might even cure some forms of blindness. The inside of the eye is coated with a thin, black layer called the **retina**. The retina is packed with special light-sensitive cells called **photoreceptors**. There are two kinds

Genetically engineered fluorescent green pigs like the one above are used to study human diseases.

of photoreceptors: rods and cones. Rods detect low levels of light at night or in the dark and are responsible for black-and-white vision. Cones detect colors in bright light or during the day.

When eye cells are damaged, the body cannot repair them. Eye damage can be caused by any number of things, including ultraviolet (UV) light from the sun and aging. But scientists have discovered that stem cells transplanted from the eyes of young mice into the retinas of blind mice successfully turned into healthy rod cells, restoring some vision. The discovery could lead to a cure for some types of human blindness. If healthy stem cells could be cloned from a person with damaged photoreceptors, they could be implanted into their retinas to help them see again.

Other scientists have used transgenic pigs to experiment with this eye-saving procedure. They created pigs that carried the fluorescent gene from jellyfish. The cells in the pigs' bodies glowed green. When scientists took eye cells from the fluorescent pigs and implanted them into the retinas of normal pigs with eye injuries, they could watch the glowing, healthy cells as they repaired the eyes.

Blindness can also be caused by clouding or scarring of the **cornea**, the window-like covering of the front of the eye. The cornea allows light to enter the eye and reach the photoreceptors in the retina. Italian scientists took adult stem cells from the cornea of a patient's good eye and cloned them until they formed a thin membrane. They then transplanted the healthy cells onto the damaged cornea of the patient's other eye. The damaged cornea repaired itself with the healthy cells. Until now, doctors have had to use corneas from the bodies of organ donors as transplants. Patients' eyesight was restored, but they had to take anti-rejection drugs for the rest of their lives to keep their bodies from rejecting the foreign corneas.

NEW SOURCES OF STEM CELLS

Scientists originally believed that stem cells could only be found in embryos. But subsequent research has shown that they occur in bone marrow, skin, blood, blood vessels, tooth pulp, muscles, intestines, the eye and brain, the umbilical cords of newborns, and fat. These "adult" stem cells sit

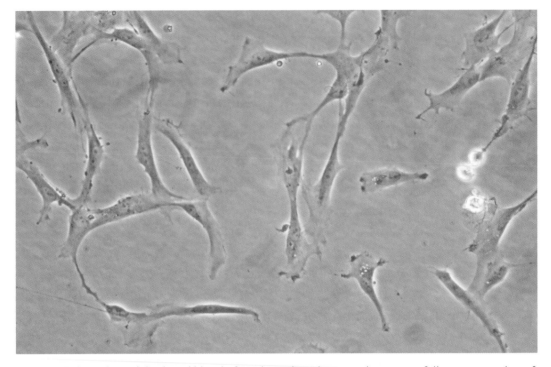

Stems cells from the umbilical cord blood of newborns have been used to successfully treat a number of diseases, eliminating the need for embryonic stem cells.

in the body, waiting to be used in case of injury or illness. Unfortunately they are not as abundant in the body as they are in embryos, so there are fewer of them to gather. And they are harder to culture than embryonic stem cells.

Fat stem cells are an exception. There are more of them in fat tissue and they are easier to extract, so harvesting them saves time and money. Veterinarians have already harvested fat stem cells from horses and used them to treat tendon, ligament, and bone injuries. The injuries heal better, faster, and with less scar tissue. Testing has shown that the method works even in horses with old or chronic injuries.

A sample of fat is removed from an injured horse and sent to a lab. The lab extracts the stem cells from the fat and places them in a syringe. A veterinarian then injects the horse's own stem cells into the injured area, triggering the healing process. The stem cells can even be frozen and stored for future treatments, if needed.

When the stem cells enter a damaged area, they transform into whatever kind of specialized cell is needed to heal the damage. They might turn into tendon, ligament, cartilage, or bone. In horses, joint injuries and bone fractures treated with stem cells healed twice as quickly as normal. Early results on treating the **degenerative** joint disease known as osteoarthritis have been positive. Even better, the treatment results in few or no side effects, so treatments for humans may be just around the corner.

Unfortunately, adult stem cells are not as versatile as embryonic stem cells. In other words, they cannot be turned into as many different kinds of cells. For example, stem cells from the brain can only be transformed into nerve cells. Stem cells from bone marrow can form blood cells and immune cells, such as white blood cells. Stem cells from the umbilical cords of newborns can create red and white blood cells, platelets for clotting blood, and bone and cartilage.

But even with limitations, adult stem cells could be useful in treating people with nerve damage or with blood diseases, such as anemia and sickle-cell anemia. Anemia is caused by a lowered red blood cell count. Sickle-cell anemia causes deformed blood cells. Both ailments result in fatigue and weakness. Scientists have already totally reversed sickle-cell anemia in mice using skin stem cells. Over time, the techniques of finding, harvesting, and cloning stem cells will be improved, and more possibilities for curing human diseases will be revealed.

A scientist extracts frozen cell cultures from a vat of liquid nitrogen.

Stem cells that are found in early human embryos are at the center of the controversy on cloning.

CHAPTER 4

Is It Right?

Cloning is the topic of a great deal of debate. Should it be "anything goes"? Should it never be done? Should DNA cloning be allowed but not reproductive cloning? What are the moral and ethical concerns? Is it safe? Because cloning is an emerging science, many questions cannot yet be answered. Sound arguments exist on both sides.

DO NOT DO IT

Two of the primary arguments against cloning have to do with morals and religion. Both act as guidelines for what is right and what is wrong. Many argue that people do not have the moral right to create life, to "play God," especially when it comes to creating humans. The Vatican, which is the center of government for the Roman Catholic Church, has denounced human cloning, saying that it is immoral, although not all Roman Catholics agree. But even people who are not particularly religious may feel that cloning is wrong because it goes against Mother Nature.

BLOG

The pope, speaking out against cloning and embryonic stem cell research:

When human beings in the weakest and most defenseless stage of their existence are selected, abandoned, killed, or used as pure 'biological matter,' how can it be denied that they are no longer being treated as 'someone' but as 'something,' thus placing the very concept of human dignity in doubt?

—Pope Benedict XVI, 2008

Pope Benedict XVI celebrates Mass.

Many people who object to cloning focus on the cloning of human embryos, whether it is to grow a few cells or to create an entire human being. They see an embryo, even when it is only a clump of a few dozen stem cells, as an individual, one with a right to its future. To remove cells from a human embryo for research does not allow that embryo to develop, and destroys its right to life. Some feel that way about all stem cell research, whether it uses human, plant, or animal cells. Others accept plant and animal stem cell research but stand against human stem cell research.

If scientists are to clone an entire human, a whole set of questions, as yet unanswerable, must be asked. How would you feel if you found out you were a clone? Would clones be discriminated against? Would someone in power clone humans against their will to be used for the cultivation of body parts? Could clones be created without a conscious mind, so they would not know what they were being used for? Clones themselves would have no say in the matter.

Is creating even a single cell morally wrong? Scientists have been trying for years to find out the minimum requirements for life. Using synthetic genes produced in a lab, they are trying to create a unicellular or single-celled organism with the least number of genes possible that will still allow it to live. The synthetic genes are pieced together and placed inside of an empty yeast cell.

That does not even take into account concerns about creating something so small that it might be capable of infecting humans. No one can predict what would happen if a newly created organism escaped into the environment, although researchers claim that the cells are designed so they would not be able to survive outside of a laboratory.

Scientists want to continue the work because once they have a minimal organism, they can add one new gene at a time to the organism so it will perform special functions, such as producing medicines or hydrogen for fuel. They could design an organism to clean up pollution, although the same concerns would exist about releasing it into the wild. Many worry that the technology could be used the wrong way, such as for making biological weapons that could harm people and the environment.

Blurring the Lines

The creation of transgenic animals that carry a different species' genes or even human genes has raised a few eyebrows. At what point does an animal become a human if it is carrying human genes? Thousands of mice, cows,

A cloned pig carries both pig and human DNA. Scientists hope to use such transgenic pigs to grow organs for transplanting into humans.

pigs, and other animals already carry human genes. Does that make them human?

Although scientists have not yet created transgenic humans that carry animal or plant genes, they have used bacterial and viral DNA to carry genes into humans. Does that make such people a human-bacterium or human-virus hybrid? Actually, this already happens in nature. Whenever a human is infected with a virus, such as the virus that causes cold sores, the virus always injects its DNA into human cells, where it becomes a permanent part of the human's DNA. Would injecting a mouse or rabbit gene into a human be any different?

Scientists have already inserted the entire nucleus from the cell of a human into the empty egg of a rabbit and grown stem cells from it. All of

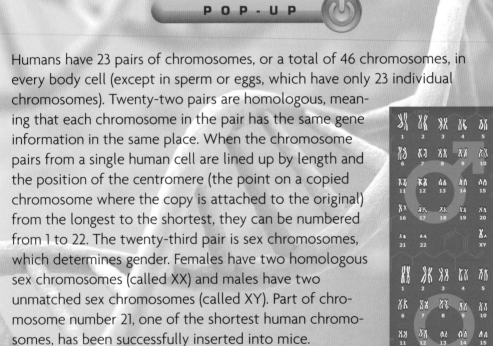

P O P - U P

Humans have 23 pairs of chromosomes, or a total of 46 chromosomes, in every body cell (except in sperm or eggs, which have only 23 individual chromosomes). Twenty-two pairs are homologous, meaning that each chromosome in the pair has the same gene information in the same place. When the chromosome pairs from a single human cell are lined up by length and the position of the centromere (the point on a copied chromosome where the copy is attached to the original) from the longest to the shortest, they can be numbered from 1 to 22. The twenty-third pair is sex chromosomes, which determines gender. Females have two homologous sex chromosomes (called XX) and males have two unmatched sex chromosomes (called XY). Part of chromosome number 21, one of the shortest human chromosomes, has been successfully inserted into mice.

Two human karyotypes (chromosome maps). Look at the 23rd pair of chromosomes in each karyotype. Which came from a female? Which came from a male?

the DNA may have been human, but the DNA in the mitochondria of the egg was certainly all rabbit, blurring the line between human and animal. And scientists are planning to introduce the "glowing" jellyfish gene into human embryos as markers for tracing development. By using the gene to target a particular cell, they would be able to watch and understand the development of specific organs as the embryo aged. Besides this being unnatural, another argument against creating transgenic humans is that it undermines human dignity, making humans less than what they are.

Is It Really Safe?

Safety is a big issue when it comes to cloning. Clones from the same donor are all susceptible to the same diseases, so an entire herd of cloned cattle or an entire cloned crop could be wiped out at once, resulting in food short-ages. One of the reasons so many species of plants and animals reproduce sexually is that it increases **genetic diversity**, the variation that is found in

Genetic diversity, as in these varieties of beans, strengthens a species' ability to survive when changes in the environment occur.

the genes of a particular species or population. The greater the genetic diversity in a species, the greater the likelihood that the species will survive changes in the environment, including exposure to disease.

Although scientists have successfully cloned many different kinds of plants and animals, many more clones have died than survived. It took more than 270 tries to create Dolly, the cloned sheep. And although scientists are getting better at it, there are still more failures than successes.

Recently, when the first dog was cloned, scientists revealed that only 2 out of 123 attempts ended with a puppy being born, and one of them died soon after birth from pneumonia. Not only are people concerned about the welfare of cloned animals, but also when it comes to pets they feel there are already too many unwanted dogs and cats in the world to warrant the continuation of pet cloning.

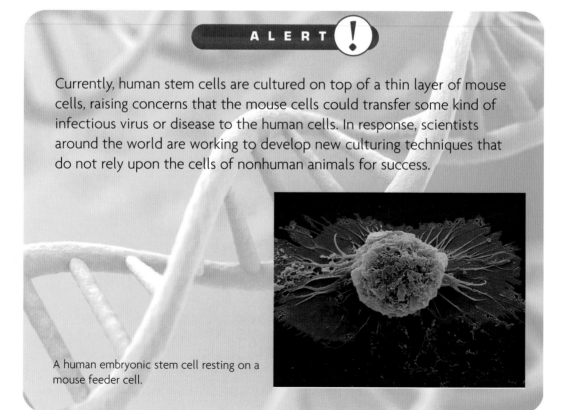

A L E R T !

Currently, human stem cells are cultured on top of a thin layer of mouse cells, raising concerns that the mouse cells could transfer some kind of infectious virus or disease to the human cells. In response, scientists around the world are working to develop new culturing techniques that do not rely upon the cells of nonhuman animals for success.

A human embryonic stem cell resting on a mouse feeder cell.

The cell membrane covering the outside of a cell acts as a barrier between the inside of a cell and the cell's environment.

CELL MEMBRANE

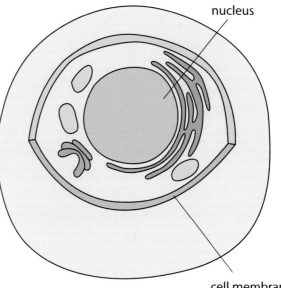

nucleus

cell membrane

In addition, cells are very fragile. They are surrounded by a thin covering called the **cell membrane**, which can break, killing the cell. DNA also fractures and breaks easily, thus destroying gene messages. The cells that survive the cloning process do not always work properly, causing deformities, disease, or death.

Embryonic stem cells that are stimulated chemically to make different kinds of cells sometimes form tumors or even make the wrong kinds of tissues. If stem cells injected into a patient's diseased heart in order to grow new blood vessels turned instead into bone, the outcome for the patient could be devastating. Many people feel the risk is simply not worth it.

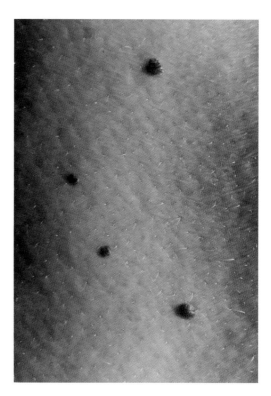

Cancerous tumors of the skin can be caused by damaged DNA that malfunctions.

There is also the question of early aging in clones. Certainly the DNA of a clone made from an adult cell is older than the DNA of a clone made from a new stem cell, but whether the former has a shorter life because of this is not yet known. Dolly the sheep, who was made from an adult cell, did die at an earlier age than expected for sheep, but whether that was due to the cloning process is not known.

Many people are concerned about the safety of food products that have been produced by genetically engineered plants and animals. Corn, tomatoes, potatoes, wheat, and many other common foods have already had their genes tinkered with. Those concerned with the environment have worried that genetically altered crops may crossbreed with closely related plants and jeopardize wild populations.

Many people believe that labeling should be used to notify consumers whether a product includes genetically modified ingredients or not.

Many cattle have been genetically engineered to boost milk production or to produce more and better quality meat. Some wonder if these altered products, both plant and animal, are safe to eat. As a precaution, some countries, such as Canada, have banned the sale of dairy products that come from genetically engineered cows. Other countries, including the United States, want all genetically modified foods to be clearly labeled so that people have a choice about whether to eat them or not.

Finally, cloning is expensive and requires special expertise. Many feel that the money spent on cloning would be better spent pursuing other methods for learning about the body and curing disease. Cloning services offered to the public, such as those that allow people to clone their cats, can only be afforded by the wealthy. If humans were to be cloned, would only the rich and powerful be able to do it? Would they clone themselves, or an army of super-humans? Although it sounds fantastic, the reality that it could happen is enough to frighten many people.

DO IT

Many people believe that the technological and medical benefits of cloning outweigh any moral or safety risks. While some say it is immoral to use human embryos for research, others say it would be immoral not to use them to save the lives of those who are already living. While some say that cloning is not natural, others argue that cloning is natural because it occurs all the time in many organisms, such as bacteria, yeast, plants, worms, snails, lizards, and even humans when they produce identical twins.

Giving Life

One of the biggest arguments in favor of cloning has to do with medical advances. Cloning is viewed as a way to literally change a person's genes to make them healthier or cure a disease. A man who cannot walk because he has been paralyzed in an accident could one day walk again. Scientists might find a way to stop out-of-control cell division, which could lead to a

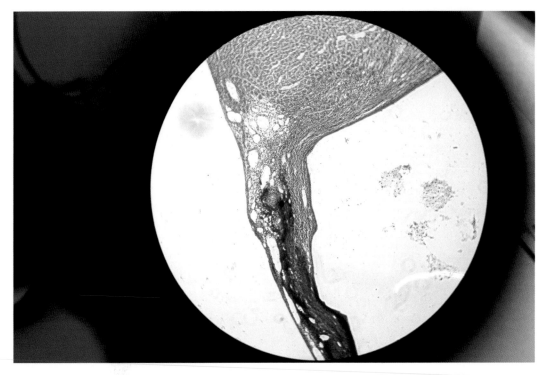

Human heart stem cells *(stained blue)* have been used to repair rat heart cells *(stained pink)* that were damaged from a heart attack. Doctors hope the method can be used to treat human heart attack victims in the near future.

cure for cancer. People would be able to age without their hearts giving out or their brains losing their ability to think cohesively.

Therapeutic and reproductive cloning has already helped hundreds of people who have been treated for serious injuries or cured of diseases. As techniques improve, people could be healthier and live longer lives. Through cloning, scientists have already gained a far better understanding of how genes, cells, tissues, organs, and the bodies of living things work.

Cloning would be particularly valuable in understanding human reproduction and helping people who are unable to have children. Couples who face the risk of passing a birth defect on to a child could have their fertilized eggs cloned in the lab and tested for any diseases or disorders. Healthy embryos could then be chosen to be implanted back into the mother, increasing the couple's chances of having a healthy child.

BLOG

Actor Christopher Reeve, best known for his role as Superman, spoke with CNN senior White House correspondent John King about his support for embryonic stem cell research. Reeve was paralyzed from the neck down when he was thrown from a horse during a cross-country event in 1995. Reeve has since died of his injuries, before stem cell advances were able to help him:

> I suffer from something called demyelination. And that means that, in one very small segment of my spinal cord, about the width of your pinky, the coating myelin, which is like the rubber coating around a wire, has come off. And that keeps signals from the brain from getting down into the body. So the human embryonic stem cells could be cultured and then sent right to the site, and they would know that their job was to remyelinate. And then the signals from the brain would go down properly, and I would get recovery of function.
>
> —Christopher Reeve, CNN Late Edition, 2001

Actor and activist Christopher Reeve, co-founder of the Christopher and Dana Reeve Paralysis Resource Center, often spoke out in favor of stem cell research, which shows promise in helping victims of paralysis and other injuries.

If human cloning ever became a reality, a woman could have a single egg (whether fertilized naturally or in a lab) collected and cloned to create several copies (twins or triplets). She could then choose to have more than one embryo implanted at one time, allowing her to have all of her children at the same time. She might choose to implant only one embryo at a time, freezing and saving the clones if needed for the future. In that case, one twin could be born years later than another twin. And, strange as it may seem, cloning would allow parents who cannot have children, but want a child that shares their genes, to clone themselves.

One parent would only have to donate a single skin cell and have all of the DNA removed and placed in an empty egg. Through **sexual reproduction**, children already receive half of each parent's DNA when they are created naturally, so some argue that it would not be that different for the child to receive the entire DNA from one parent. The parent would essentially have a delayed identical twin of him- or herself. However, the child would be born at a different time, have different experiences, be exposed to a different environment, and develop a different personality. Anyone who knows identical twins that were produced the natural way knows that they are not exactly alike. Their genes may be identical, but each is a unique individual.

Parents might even be able to choose the genes of their children or engineer them to have particular traits, perhaps a certain hair color or even greater intelligence. Of course, because of the environment and children's experiences as they grow, this would not guarantee another Einstein.

Modifying Livestock and Crops

Animals, such as pigs, might be able to grow organs that could be used as replacement parts for people. Organs could be mass-produced so that peo-

Identical twins *(left)* are genetically identical, but unique in personality, experiences, and often in likes and dislikes. Two brothers *(right)* were conceived at the same time, but born four years apart. The younger boy's embryo was kept frozen until it was implanted later into the mother.

ple, who now wait years for a transplant, hoping to get one before they die, could get one right away. Pig hearts are very similar to human hearts, so scientists have been working to knock out the gene that would cause the human body to reject one if it were transplanted into a human.

Those who argue for cloning like the idea of increasing food yields by genetically engineering crops to be resistant to drought or disease or by modifying cows to produce more milk or meat. They point out that, so far, no harm has come to anyone who has eaten modified food. After all, people eat DNA all the time. It is in every cell of every piece of fruit, vegetable, or meat that we eat already. And all of those foods have been genetically modified to make them bigger, sweeter, or juicier through **selective breeding** for hundreds of years. Cloning would simply speed things up.

To opponents of embryonic stem cell research, proponents point out that with the discovery of adult stem cells in animals, including humans, stem cells from embryos may no longer be needed. Although adult stem cells do not seem to be as versatile as embryonic stem cells, because they cannot be changed into as many different kinds of cells, they are certainly a good alternative.

Scientists in the United States and Japan recently figured out how to insert four specific genes into the skin cells of mice, which changed the skin cells back into what appeared to be embryonic stem cells. If the cells turn out to be what they seem, the potential for creating embryonic stem cells without actually destroying human embryos would revolutionize the science of stem cell research.

A scientist tests DNA samples for variations in genes that might indicate a person's susceptibility to certain forms of cancer.

CHAPTER 5

What Does
the Future Hold?

Whether or not you agree with cloning, it is here to stay. New advances in DNA, therapeutic, and reproductive cloning are being made every day. Some predict that these advances will lead to cures for diabetes, cancer, and a host of other diseases within the next ten to twenty years. Gene therapy could become commonplace. There are numerous possible applications of cloning technology that until now were beyond our wildest imagination.

It begins with **diagnostics**, one of the fastest growing fields in genetics. Gene diagnostics is the science of identifying diseases that are caused by genes. Once a disease gene is identified, treatments can be recommended. Diagnostics can also identify a person's potential for contracting a particular disease, often years in advance. Changes can then be made in diet or lifestyle to reduce the chances of ever developing the disease.

NEW KINDS OF STEM CELLS

One of the most promising new developments in cloning research has been the discovery of stem cells in adult organisms. If adult stem cells could

TOOL BAR

A number of companies provide services for diagnosing genetic diseases. Automated systems known as gene-reading machines work quickly to scan a person's genes using only a single drop of blood. A computer then prints out a list that identifies both weaknesses and strengths in the genes, such as tendencies to either get or resist certain kinds of cancer. You may one day be able to get a complete gene printout as easily as you can get a credit card. One precaution, though: Experts expect that new laws will need to be made to protect people from discrimination if it is known that they carry a gene for a disease.

be used for research, embryos would no longer be needed, which would eliminate one of the strongest objections to cloning. However, adult stem cells cannot be changed into as many different kinds of cells as embryonic stem cells, so their use is limited at this time. Scientists hope that new technologies will change that. For example, scientists in the United States recently discovered a new kind of bone marrow cell that can turn into almost as many different kinds of body cells as embryonic stem cells.

Because of objections to the creation of human embryos for scientific study, many other scientists are working with old cell lines that were started from embryos collect-

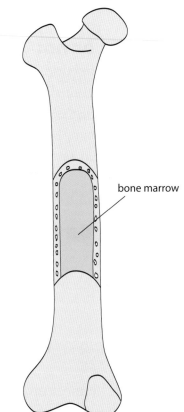

section of bone showing marrow

bone marrow

Stem cells found in bone marrow, the soft tissue inside of bones, can give rise to a variety of different kinds of body cells, including white blood cells, red blood cells, bone cells, and muscle cells.

ed years ago. These cell lines have the advantage of being able to reproduce consistently (without developing abnormalities) and are known to be free of all human, mouse, pig, and cow viruses. Because stem cells have historically been grown on a thin layer of animal cells, the transfer of viruses from one species to another has long been a concern.

Companies specializing in these "clean" stem cell lines are cropping up around the world. Cells from various lines are producing human heart cells, liver cells, pancreatic cells that produce insulin to fight diabetes, and nerve cells, including the type of brain cells that are lost in people who have Parkinson's disease. People with Parkinson's have trouble moving and speaking. If their damaged nerve cells could be replaced by stem cells, they might regain those lost functions.

Stem cells that consistently change into nerve cells may also one day improve movement in people with spinal injuries or even cure paralysis. Scientists have already cured paralysis in a rat that was unable to move its hind legs. The damaged cells in the spine were replaced with healthy stem cells, and the rat walked again, with only a slight shuffle.

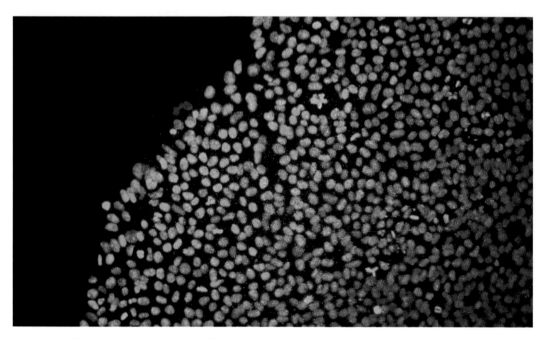

A colony of human embryonic stem cells grown without the help of mouse feeder cells, which have been known to contaminate human cells.

A CURE FOR CANCER

Hundreds of thousands of people die each year in the United States from cancer. There are many different kinds of cancer, depending on which type of tissue a specific cancer is found in. Almost all are caused by abnormalities in genes. It is interesting that cancer is actually caused by a person's own body cells that begin multiplying out of control, invading tissues, forming tumors, and sometimes spreading throughout the body.

Cancer results when the genes that control normal cell reproduction and growth no longer function properly. The defective genes might be caused by something in the environment, such as exposure to poisons or radiation, or they might be inherited or passed down from a parent (if the gene abnormalities occur in sperm or eggs). Left untreated, invading cancer

Advances in stem cell research might one day eliminate the need for patients to undergo debilitating chemotherapy.

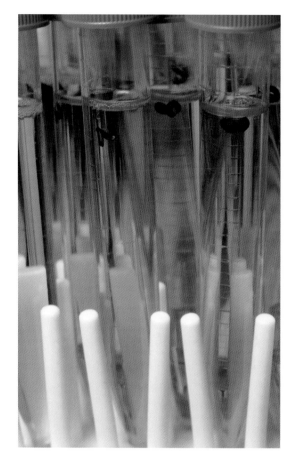

By combining the DNA of two different types of cells—one that grows continuously and another that makes a particular kind of anti-body—scientists are able to produce large amounts of pure antibodies (*right*) for use in cancer research.

cells damage normal cells in the body, eventually causing organ failure and death. Cancer affects people of all ages and back-grounds.

Traditional cancer treatments include surgery, chemotherapy, and radiation therapy, depending on the type and severity of the cancer. If they have not spread throughout the body, cancer masses can be removed through surgery. Chemotherapy uses chemicals or drugs to target the cancer by blocking cell division and, hope-fully, stopping the out-of-control cells in their tracks. Radiation uses X-rays to damage the genes in the cancer cells, so they can no longer give instructions to continue growing. The goal is to destroy the cancer cells without destroying too many of the body's healthy cells at the same time.

Because these traditional treatments also kill normal cells, their side effects include pain, bleeding, vomiting, diarrhea, weakness, and hair loss. Gene and stem cell therapies, however, do not cause these symptoms. Gene therapies have already been used to cure brain and pancreatic cancer in mice.

To cure brain tumors in mice, scientists genetically alter mouse cells to contain a harmless virus. The virus carries a gene that produces a special pro-tein that is toxic only to cancer cells. When the mouse cells are injected into brain tumors, the virus gene produces the protein, which kills cancer cells but leaves normal cells undamaged. The brain tumors are completely destroyed.

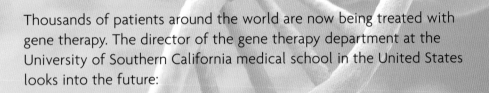

Thousands of patients around the world are now being treated with gene therapy. The director of the gene therapy department at the University of Southern California medical school in the United States looks into the future:

Twenty years from now gene therapy will
have revolutionized the practice of medicine.
Virtually every disease will have gene therapy as one of its treatments.

—Dr. W. French Anderson, University of Southern California, 1999

Gene therapy has also prevented the onset of a brain disorder called Huntington's disease, at least in cultures of cells in the lab. Huntington's causes people to lose the ability to think and reason clearly. Scientists placed genes that strengthen brain cells into the empty cases of viruses (with the virus DNA removed). The viruses could no longer use cells to reproduce more viruses, but they still injected the strengthening genes into brain cells. The new genes fortified the brain cells and blocked the development of the

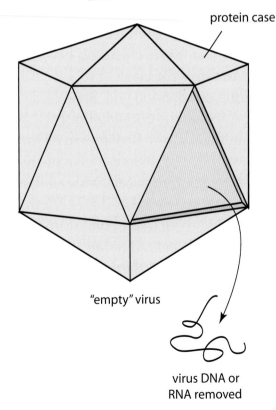

EMPTY VIRUS

protein case

"empty" virus

virus DNA or RNA removed

By removing virus DNA from a virus and inserting desirable genes, scientists can use the virus to deliver gene treatments into diseased cells.

disease. Scientists have also tested altered viruses that only target specific brain cancer cells, killing them but leaving healthy brain cells alone.

Similar trials for humans with cancer have already begun. In 2006, two people were cured of a particularly deadly cancer that had spread throughout their bodies. First, their blood was drawn and their white blood cells—the disease-fighters of the body—were removed. Then the white blood cells were genetically altered using a virus to insert new genes that make the white blood cells capable of identifying the specific cancer cells. Finally, the altered white blood cells were injected back into the patients' bodies, where they went to work obliterating all traces of the deadly cancer.

While the therapy did not work in every patient who was treated, the technique holds great promise for curing many kinds of cancer in the future. Because a patient's own cells are used, the body does not reject them when they are reinjected. Best of all, the cancer is treated without the horrible side effects caused by traditional cancer therapies.

A PRESCRIPTION FOR GENES

Scientists predict that within the next few decades, doctors will be able to design personalized, gene-based medicines to treat most common diseases. Drugs will be mass-produced in genetically engineered bacteria and animals. Potentially, a cow clone could be manufactured that would hold a patient's own genes and produce a specific product needed by that individual. The cow could make antibodies to fight a particular disease, growth hormones to help promote growth, reproductive hormones needed to have a child, or even proteins to slow the aging process.

Diseases such as arthritis could also become a thing of the past. Arthritis destroys the joints of people as they age, causing pain, swelling, and deformities. But in one experiment, scientists replaced the genes of a virus with human genes that block inflammation and joint damage. When the modified viruses were injected into the joints of arthritis patients, their symptoms were relieved after just one treatment.

Another experiment used genetically modified cells, which were injected into joints to encourage cartilage growth. New cartilage replaced the

Three cloned calves have been genetically engineered to produce human antibodies.

cartilage that had worn away. The loss of cartilage and bone in the joints of aging people causes grinding and inflammation, so there is hope not only to relieve the symptoms of arthritis but to cure it altogether.

Another human disease called multiple sclerosis, or MS, causes muscle weakness and eventually paralysis. The damage is caused when a patient's own immune system mistakenly attacks the nerves that control muscles. Scientists have now identified some of the genes that contribute to MS. If gene therapies can be modified to block the malfunctioning genes, a cure for MS could soon be developed.

People suffering from mental illness, such as schizophrenia or depression, may also find treatments or cures through gene therapies. Scientists have already discovered that by altering a single gene in antisocial mice, the mice became friendlier, spending more time interacting, nuzzling, and grooming with their fellow mice. The mice were given a gene from anoth-

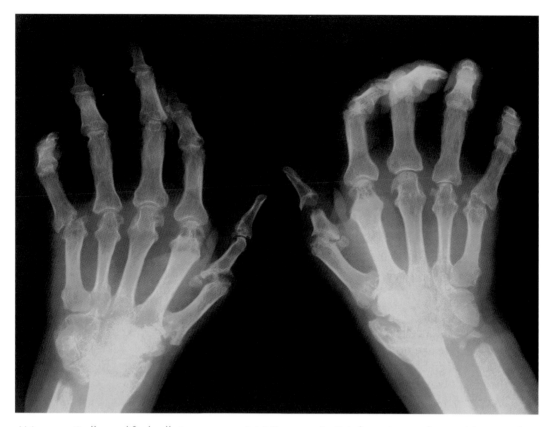

Using genetically modified cells to grow new joint tissues, scientists hope to one day provide a cure for the deforming and painful disease called arthritis.

er rodent called the prairie vole. Prairie voles live in colonies on grasslands in the central United States and show a number of social behaviors that are very similar to humans. Could such a gene help humans in the same way?

Another group of U.S. scientists has removed stem cells from the brain of a human and transplanted them into the brain of a mouse. The human cells started working right alongside the mouse cells. The scientists hope that the same technology could be used to renew human brains when they have been damaged by severe injury, such as in an automobile accident, or degraded by disease, such as Alzheimer's disease. Alzheimer's is a degenerative disease of the brain, particularly in the elderly, which robs people of the ability to think normally and perform even the simplest daily tasks.

Scientists in the United States have developed a new approach to gene therapy that they hope will one day cure acquired immune deficiency syndrome, or AIDS. AIDS kills thousands of people every year, and while doctors can now delay symptoms with drugs, there is no cure. AIDS is a sexually transmitted disease, which can also be spread through contact with infected blood, such as when drug users share the same needles to inject drugs. It is caused by the human immunodeficiency virus (HIV), which destroys cells in the body's immune system. People with AIDS have trouble fighting off disease. Early testing shows that the new therapy works by preventing the HIV virus from entering and destroying those immune-system cells:

To penetrate a cell, HIV needs two receptors that operate like door knobs and allow the virus inside. HIV grabs the receptor and forces itself into the cell. If we can knock out one of these receptors, we hoped to prevent HIV from infecting the cell.

—David Baltimore, Nobel laureate, California Institute of Technology, 2002

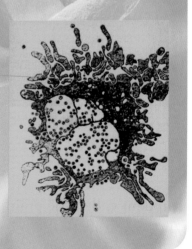

HIV *(small dots)* invading a white blood cell.

ANIMAL-TO-HUMAN TRANSPLANTS

With the advances made in producing transgenic animals, it may not be long before organs are regularly grown for human transplant. Animals could be custom-designed to carry an individual's DNA for making a particular organ. The organ could be ready and waiting as a replacement, should it ever be needed. A cow could grow a new liver for someone with hepatitis, a type of liver disease. A pig could grow new skin for a person with severe burns. A dog could grow a new bladder for someone with bladder cancer.

In 2006, U.S. scientists created one of the first cloned livers from embryonic stem cells in mice, which were mixed with human liver cells inside a special bag. Most of the stem cells turned into functioning liver cells. When the artificial livers were implanted into mice with liver failure, they took over the duties of the damaged liver and functioned normally. Scientists have also grown functioning artificial kidneys under the skin of cows, providing hope for future kidney transplant patients.

U.S. scientists have successfully grown bladders in the lab, transplanting them first into dogs and then, in 2006, into humans. They started by taking cells from a patient's bladder and spreading them onto a collagen frame. Collagen is a protein found in the connective tissue of **vertebrates**. The implanted cells grew over the frame to form the new bladder.

Because a person's diseased organ often cannot provide enough healthy cells to seed such a structure, scientists hope to use stem cells that can be chemically stimulated to form all of the different kinds of tissue necessary to form a functioning bladder ready for transplant. The technology could then be applied to growing other body organs.

CROPS, LIVESTOCK, AND THE ENVIRONMENT

Some scientists predict that eventually all crops and livestock grown for human consumption will be genetically engineered to make them "better" in some way. Corn that has been genetically engineered to resist pests, such as corn earworms, is already commonly used because it is cheaper to produce. A gene from another plant, which makes a protein that is toxic to harmful insects but not to people, is inserted into the corn's cells.

Farmers save money planting genetically engineered corn because they do not have to buy chemicals to spray their crops. They also do not have to pay for fuel to run the equipment to spray the chemicals. Traditional corn crops require more land for planting because worms that survive spraying destroy a large number of ears of corn. In addition, traditional corn has to

A new, genetically engineered variety of rice has been developed to withstand the flooding that regularly destroys rice crops around the world.

be partly or completely shucked to remove any infestations of earworms before it is sent to market, adding even more to the cost. Although many people are concerned that genetically engineered crops might not be safe, consumer studies have shown that when modified food is labeled (which is voluntary in the United States), people do not avoid buying it.

A number of crops, including soybeans and cotton, are commonly engineered to resist pests or disease, but a new gene—dubbed by some the "waterproof" gene—that was recently discovered might help protect the world's rice crop. Any rice modified with the new gene would be able to survive flooding in the wet climates where it is grown. Flooding regularly destroys many rice crops. Preliminary tests have shown that the modified rice can survive underwater ten times as long as traditional rice.

It will not be long before other crops are genetically engineered to

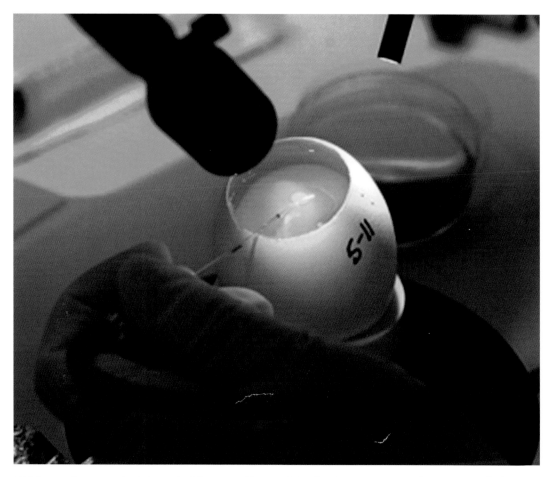

Chicken embryos can be injected with stem cells containing foreign genes to produce meatier chickens, better layers, or even to produce better medicines for humans.

increase yields. In 2007, farmers announced they would soon begin growing beets that have been engineered to resist weed killers. That way they can spray their crops to kill weeds without killing the crop in the process.

Genetically engineered livestock could become more common than not. Chickens have already been modified to produce a double punch. Right now, "meaty" chickens that are bred for the meat market do not make good egg layers. "Layer" chickens that are bred for laying eggs do not make good meat. So, scientists implanted the genes of the meaty chickens into the eggs of the layer chickens. The chicks that hatched grew into meaty chickens that laid lots of eggs. When the altered chickens pass their

Scientists are in the process of engineering bacteria to digest toxic wastes. The bacteria could then be used to clean up pollutants in the environment.

peak in egg laying, they can still be used for meat. Who knows what is in store for pigs, goats, and any number of other farm animals?

Work is even under way to genetically modify bacteria to help clean up the environment. Scientists have totally changed one species of bacterium into another by doing a complete gene swap. The new genes completely replaced the old genes and began working properly. Called a "genome transplant," scientists consider this the first step toward creating artificial bacteria that can break down oil resulting from an oil spill, clean pollutants out of the air, turn sewage into fresh water, or even produce a clean fuel that could run automobiles and factories. The bacteria could be designed with specific genes to do their jobs.

In the future, the umbilical cord of every child might be frozen at the time of birth. The umbilical cord is the tube that connects a baby's bloodstream to its mother when it is in the uterus. It is rich in stem cells that could be saved for a rainy day, when the person might need those cells to cure a disease or heal an injury. Because people would have their own cells to harvest, any possibility of cell, tissue, or organ rejection would be eliminated.

DESIGNER BABIES

Made-to-order babies could soon become a reality. With advances in genetic engineering, parents would be able to select the genes that they want passed on to their children. In a procedure called genetic selection, scientists insert genes into a fertilized egg and perhaps remove others. In this way, parents might be able to make their babies more intelligent or athletic, taller, or less likely to get diseases, such as cancer. They might be able to remove a genetic mutation that might cause a birth defect or disease.

Once a fertilized egg has been modified and it begins to divide, new cells will be formed. Because cells pass on their genetic information when they reproduce or divide, every new cell in the new baby will carry the gene modifications. When the child is grown, he or she would also be able to pass on those new genes to the next generation.

BRING THEM BACK

Have you ever seen a black rhinoceros, a giant panda, or a gaur? Few people have. These are a few of the most endangered species on Earth. Cloning could help bring them back. In 2001, the gaur, a wild ox from India, was one of the first endangered species to be cloned.

This gaur, a type of wild ox, was the first endangered species to be cloned.

Forty cloned gaur embryos were created by inserting gaur DNA into empty cow eggs. The embryos were then implanted into cows. Eight pregnancies resulted, but only one baby gaur was born. Unfortunately, the gaur died two days later from an infection that was not believed to be related to its cloning.

The gaur's birth did prove, however, that cloning endangered species was possible. Since then, scientists have cloned an endangered species of sheep called the mouflon, which is found on several islands in the Mediterranean. Using cells from the eggs of an adult female mouflon that had died, they transferred the mouflon DNA into empty sheep eggs and implanted them into sheep. Finally, a baby mouflon was born, also in 2001, and, unlike the gaur, the baby survived.

A number of institutions around the world are now collecting cells and tissues from as many disappearing species as they can. The cells are frozen for use in the future. As cloning technology is improved, scientists might be able to use these "frozen zoos" as tools to ensure that many of the earth's unique species do not disappear forever.

The cells of endangered animals are stored in frozen zoos with the hope that new technologies in the future will help to bring them back.

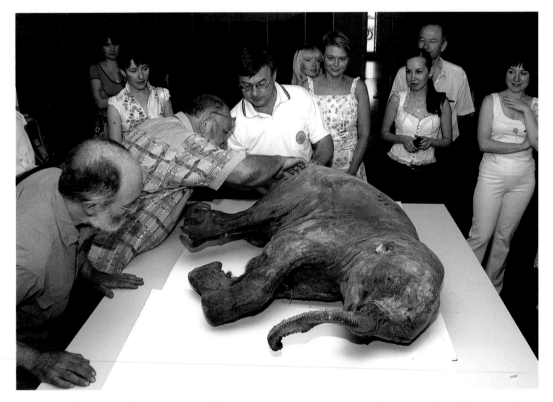

A frozen baby mammoth discovered in Siberia has prompted some scientists to wonder if cloning technology could be used to bring back extinct species.

Even more unusual is the effort to bring back extinct species such as the quagga, a zebralike animal; the Tasmanian tiger, a small doglike marsupial; and the woolly mammoth. In recent years, the body of a frozen mammoth was discovered in Siberia. Some of its cells still contained samples of DNA. Scientists want to bring back the mammoth by inserting its DNA into the empty eggs of elephants, and then implanting the resulting embryos into female elephants. Will *Jurassic Park* become a reality? Only time will tell.

Timeline

1866
Gregor Mendel, often called the father of genetics, publishes "Experiments on Plant Hybridization" in which he outlines the basic laws on inheritance of traits in pea plants. Mendel's work lays the groundwork for later studies of genetics.

1902
German scientist Hans Spemann created the first artificial clone in his laboratory by using a human hair to split a two-celled salamander embryo into two individual cells.

1903
Herbert Weber, from the U.S. Department of Agriculture, coined the word "clone," derived from the Greek word meaning twig.

1928
Spemann performs the first nuclear transfer using embryonic cells.

1944
Oswald Avery, a Canadian-born American physician and medical researcher, discovers that a cell's genetic information is carried in DNA and not in cell protein as was earlier believed.

1952
The first true clone was created when scientists removed the nucleus from a frog egg and replaced it with a nucleus taken from a developing frog embryo.

1953
While working at the Cambridge Cavendish Laboratory, Francis Crick and James Watson, using x-rays taken by Rosalind Franklin, build the first model of the structure of DNA.

1960s
Scientists use the adult body cells of frogs to perform nuclear transfers.

1990s
Large numbers of mice are cloned for research.

1990
In October, The National Institutes of Health, headed by James Watson, officially launched the Human Genome Project.

Jurassic Park, a science fiction novel written by Michael Crichton, is published. It describes an amusement park featuring genetically created dinosaurs.

1993
Jurassic Park is adapted into a blockbuster film, with two more movies to follow: *Lost World* (1995) and *Jurassic Park III* (2001).

1996
Dolly the sheep is the first mammal to be cloned from an adult cell. She was created by Ian Wilmut and Keith Cambell at the Roslin Institute in Scotland.

1997
Scientists grow a human-shaped ear out of cow cartilage, which is then successfully transplanted onto the back of a mouse.

The first cloned mouse is born at the University of Hawaii medical school. It is the first of fifty identical mouse clones to be created from a single adult mouse.

1998
Dolly gives birth to a lamb named Bonnie. Although Dolly was a clone, Bonnie was conceived naturally. The first cow is cloned at the University of Connecticut.

2000
British scientists clone the first pig, and Chinese scientists clone the first goat.

2001
Scientists at Texas A&M University successfully clone the first domestic cat, creating CC (short for Copy Cat).

The gaur, a wild ox from India, is the first endangered species to be cloned.

2002
French scientists clone the first rabbit.

2003
Dolly, the first mammal clone, dies. A cloned mule, the first clone of the horse family, is born at the University of Idaho. Soon after, Italian scientists announce the birth of the first cloned horse.

2005
Scientists in South Korea clone the first domestic dog, Snuppy (short for Seoul National University puppy).

2006
U.S. scientists create one of the first cloned livers.

2008
The U.S. Food and Drug Administration (FDA) announces that meat and milk from cloned pigs, cattle, and goats are safe to eat.

Scientists at a U.S. company announce that they have cloned the first mature human embryos.

Glossary

antibodies—special proteins released by white blood cells in the blood that help destroy bacteria, viruses, or other particles that can make you sick

asexual reproduction—type of reproduction in which offspring come from a single parent, and inherit only the genes of that parent

bacteria (*singular*, bacterium)—extremely small, single-celled organisms without a nucleus; prokaryotes

cell culture—the growth of cells in an artificial medium for experimental purposes; cells that are grown outside of a living organism

cell membrane—a thin layer around the outside of a cell that acts as a barrier between the inside of the cell and the cell's environment, and controls what enters and leaves the cell

clone—a cell or organism that is genetically identical to the cell or organism from which it was made

cornea—a clear protective covering over the front of the eye that allows light to enter

degenerative—causing the breakdown of tissues or organs until they can no longer work properly

diabetes—a disease caused when the body does not make enough of the hormone insulin, which is used by body cells to take in sugar from the blood and use it for energy

diagnostics—the science of identifying a disease from its signs and symptoms

differentiated—having developed different characteristics

embryo—an animal in the earliest stage of development; in plants, called a sporophyte

extract—to remove or take out of

fluorescent—glowing; fluorescence is caused by the change of one kind of light into a bright, shimmering light

genetic diversity—the variations that are found in the genes of living things, including within or between populations, within individuals of the same species, or among many different species

genetic engineering—the manipulation of a gene or genes in an organism with the aim of introducing new characteristics

homologous—the name for chromosomes that pair during meiosis; homologous chromosomes are the same size and have genes located in the same place (but do not necessarily have the same alleles on those genes)

hormone—a chemical produced by special glands in the body, which speeds up or slows down the activities of a tissue or organ

mammalian—belonging to the group of warm-blooded vertebrates whose young feed on milk produced by glands in the female

meiosis—cell division that produces gametes or sex cells, each with half the chromosomes of the original cell.

mitosis—cell division in which each new cell receives a copy of all the chromosomes from the original cell

nuclear transfer—a form of cloning that involves the removal of the nucleus (with all of its DNA) from a body cell and injecting it into an egg that has had its nucleus removed

organelles—structures inside a cell that carry out specific jobs for the cell.

organism—a living thing made of one or more cells that contain DNA

photoreceptors—specialized nerve cells in the retina of the eye that detect light

plasmid—a small, extra piece of circular DNA that is normally found inside a bacterial cell

premature—happening before the proper or usual time

recombinant DNA—a DNA molecule formed by the joining of genes from two different organisms

remission—the absence of the symptoms of a disease in patients with chronic illness

retina—a layer of light-sensitive cells in the back of the eye that sends nerve impulses to the brain

saliva—the watery fluid produced by glands in the mouth, which begins the breakdown of food

selective breeding—the breeding of organisms whereby humans select certain desired traits to be passed on to the next generation

sexual reproduction—reproduction involving two parents who each contribute half their genes to produce a new individual

stem cell—an unspecialized cell that can develop into any one of many different kinds of specialized cells, such as a skin cell or a nerve cell

transgenic—containing genes (DNA) that have been artificially transferred from a different organism

vertebrate—an animal with a backbone, which includes mammals, birds, reptiles, amphibians, and fish

zygote—the first cell formed after the fertilization of an egg by a sperm

Search Engine

BOOKS AND MAGAZINES

"See, Blind Mice." *Scholastic Science World* 63, no. 9 (2007).

Weiss, Rick. "The Stem Cell Divide." *National Geographic* 208, no. 1 (2005).

Wilmut, Ian, and Roger Highfield. *After Dolly: The Uses and Misuses of Human Cloning.* New York: W.W. Norton, 2006.

Zehnder, Jennifer. "Stem-Cell Research Offers New Options." *Western Horseman*, May 2007.

WEB SITES

ABC News Online
   abcnews.go.com/Technology/DyeHard/Story?id=3828064&page=1
   Dye, Lee. 2007. "Tiny Fish Reveals Cancer Secrets." *Dye Hard Science.*

Access Excellence
   www.accessexcellence.org/WN/SU/copycat.html
   Henahan, Sean. 2002. "Molecular Meow Mix Creates Copy Cat Clone." *Science News.*

Associated Press/MSNBC Technology and Science
   www.msnbc.msn.com/id/6747736/
   Elias, Paul. 2004. "Pet-Cloning Company Makes a Landmark Sale."

BBC News
   news.bbc.co.uk/2/hi/health/1949073.stm
   "Artificial Liver Could Be Grown." 2002.

BBC News Online
   news.bbc.co.uk/2/hi/science/nature/2183200.stm
   Briggs, Helen. 2002. "Cows Born with Human DNA."

Bio-Medicine.org
   news.bio-medicine.org/biology-news-2/UCLA-Caltech-scientists-develop-new-gene-therapy-approach-6008–1/
   Schmidt, Elaine. 2002. "UCLA/Cal Tech Scientists Develop New Gene Therapy Approach."

CNN TV Late Edition
   archives.cnn.com/2001/ALLPOLITICS/07/29/reeve.cnna/index.html
   2001.
   "Christopher Reeve on Politics and Stem Cell Research." *Inside Politics.*

FDA News.
www.fda.gov/bbs/topics/NEWS/2008/NEW01776.html
2008. "FDA Issues Documents on the Safety of Food from Animal Clones."

Genome News Network
www.genomenewsnetwork.org/articles/10_01/cloned_sheep.shtml
Winstead, Edward R. 2001. "Endangered Wild Sheep Clone Reported to Be Healthy."

Human Genome Project
www.ornl.gov/sci/techresources/Human_Genome/elsi/cloning.shtml
"Cloning Fact Sheet."

National Geographic News
news.nationalgeographic.com/news/2005/08/0803_050803_dog_clone.html
Mott, Maryann. 2005. "Dog Cloned by South Korean Scientists."

NewScientist.com.
www.newscientist.com/article/dn982-clones-contain-hidden-DNA-damage.html
Coghlan, Andy. 2001. "Clones Contain Hidden DNA Damage." News Service.

NewScientist.com.
www.newscientist.com/article/dn1931-cloners-create-worlds-first-copycat.html
Cohen, Philip. 2002. "Cloners Create World's First Copy-Cat." News Service.

Proceedings of the National Academy of Science online
www.pnas.org/misc/classics4/shtml
Brownlee, Christen. 2008. "Nuclear Transfer: Bringing in the Clones."

Science Clarified
www.scienceclarified.com/Ci-Co/Clone-and-Cloning.html
2007. "Clone and Cloning."

Science Daily
www.sciencedaily.com/releases/2007/07/070730111638.htm
University of Central Florida. 2007. "Insulin Grown in Plants Relieves Diabetes in Mice: Holds Promise for Humans."

Science News Online
www.sciencenews.org/articles/20010210/note14.asp
Milius, Susan. 2001. "Cloned Gaur Born Healthy, Then Dies."

The Mail Online
www.dailymail.co.uk/pages/live/articles/news/worldnews.html
Associated News Media. 2008. "Pope Condemns Human Cloning and Stem Cell Research."

Time
www.time.com/time/magazine/article/9,0171,989989–1,00.html
Jaroff, Leon. 1999. "Fixing the Genes." U.S. News.

Index

Page numbers in italics refer to illustrations.

About the Author

Susan Schafer is a science teacher and the author of several nonfiction books for children. She has written about numerous animals, including horses, snakes, tigers, Komodo dragons, and Galapagos tortoises. Her book on the latter was named an Outstanding Science Trade Book for Children by the National Science Teachers Association and Children's Book Council. She has also written a fictional book about animal tails for very young children. Schafer has spent many years working in the field of biology and enjoys sharing her knowledge and appreciation of nature with others. She lives on a ranch in Santa Margarita, California, with her husband, horses, and dogs, and with the beauty of the oak-covered hills around her.

WITHDRAWN